向梦想前进

Social Emotional and Multicultural Learning | Non-Fiction Series

Copyright © 2022 by Level Learning, INC. and Washington Yu Ying PCS™
Original and Edited Text Copyright © 2022 by Washington Yu Ying PCS™

All rights reserved. No part of this book in whole or part may be reproduced without written permission from the publisher.

Published byLevel Learning, INC.

Content Contributors:
Washington Yu Ying PCS™
Level Learning - Ya-Ching Chang

Illustrations by: Josh Taira

Leveling classification based on Level Learning standard. For full description, visit www.levellearning.com

ISBN 978-1-64040-088-7
Simplified Chinese Edition

About Level Learning:
Level Learning provides a literacy focused curriculum specifically designed for K-12 Chinese as a Second Language classrooms. Our program offers 20 levels of specific and detailed objectives, leveled texts and passages, mastery-based online assessment, and analytics to enable data-driven instruction. Level Learning reading curriculum for both literature and informational text emphasize grammar and comprehension skills to help teachers develop confident and independent Chinese language readers. The non-fiction series of books are specifically designed to support our informational text course based on multiple national standards. To learn more about our entire offering, visit www.levellearning.com.

About Washington Yu Ying PCS™:
Washington Yu Ying PCS is a Mandarin English dual language immersion International Baccalaureate (IB) World school. Yu Ying's mission is to inspire and prepare young people to create a better world by challenging them to reach their full potential in a nurturing Chinese/English educational environment. Yu Ying's comprehensive IB, dual immersion curriculum equips students with global competencies for success in the real world. As a leader in immersion education, Yu Ying is determined to advance Chinese language programs and global citizenry education by helping other schools create and strengthen their Chinese programs. For more information, email: products@washingtonyuying.org

你有没有梦想过自己成为一位球星，在球场上大展身手；或是梦想自己变成了一位歌星，在舞台上大放异彩？只要你有梦想，就应该勇敢地向梦想前进。

人们都拥有过美好的梦想，但是大部分人都没有实现他们的梦想。为什么呢？这是因为这些人只有梦想，而没有行动。

如果你的梦想是成为一位画家,但是你却不愿意花时间练习绘画,或者总是对自己没信心。那么,这个梦想只会成为空想。

空想和梦想是不同的。拥有梦想的同时，我们也要有实际的计划和行动。

首先，我们要相信自己的能力。如果想成为一位画家，每次画画的时候，不仅要对自己有信心，而且要尽自己最大的努力。

其次,我们可以制定一个计划,把一个比较难达到的目标分成几个小目标,然后一步步地去完成。

比如说，给自己设定一段时间，加强绘画的技巧，并且参加学校的绘画比赛。达到这个目标以后，再向下一个目标继续努力。只有行动起来，我们才能向梦想前进。

实现梦想的过程可能会很*漫长*。但是，这个过程会让我们收获很多，也会对自己更有信心。

你知道吗?每个成功的人,背后都有一段艰苦奋斗的故事。只要肯努力,不放弃,终有一天会梦想成真。

你的梦想是什么呢?把你的梦想写成实际的目标,然后向梦想前进吧!

Glossary

	Pinyin	English Definition
梦想	mèng xiǎng	to dream
球星	qiú xīng	sport star
大展身手	dà zhǎn shēn shǒu	to exhibit skill or talent
歌星	gē xīng	singer
舞台	wǔ tái	stage
大放异彩	dà fàng yì cǎi	to shine (of talent)
向	xiàng	to turn toward
前进	qián jìn	to go forward
大部分	dà bù fèn	in large part
实现	shí xiàn	to achieve
行动	xíng dòng	action
画家	huà jiā	painter, artist
愿意	yuàn yì	willing
花	huā	to waste

	Pinyin	English Definition
练习	liàn xí	to practice
信心	xìn xīn	confidence
空想	kōng xiǎng	daydream
实际	shí jì	practical
计划	jì huà	plan
能力	néng lì	ability
努力	nǔ lì	to work or try hard
制定	zhì dìng	to develop
难	nán	difficult
达到	dá dào	to reach
目标	mù biāo	goal
设定	shè dìng	to set
加强	jiā qiáng	to strengthen
技巧	jì qiǎo	skill, technique

Glossary

	Pinyin	English Definition
绘画	huì huà	drawing, painting
比赛	bǐ sài	competition
继续	jì xù	to continue
漫长	màn cháng	very long
奋斗	fèn dòu	struggle
放弃	fàng qì	to abandon
梦想成真	mèng xiǎng chéng zhēn	dream come true (idiom)

www.ingramcontent.com/pod-product-compliance
Lightning Source LLC
Chambersburg PA
CBHW041220070526
44584CB00001B/33